Canning and Preserving for Beginners

A Complete Step-by-Step Guide to the Art of Preserving and Canning Food with Recipes

By

MOLLY WOOLERY

Contents

Introduction

People have required the ability to preserve food from the beginning of time. Even though the process could be time and energy-consuming, it was preferable then going hungry during the winter in old times. Foods were initially preserved by smoking, drying, fermenting, or cooling/freezing (given the right type of environment). More techniques were later developed, including salt curing, pickling in an acid (like vinegar), and producing jams and jellies with honey and sugar. None of these procedures was perfect, so efforts to find faster, more dependable approaches that also made the food simple to store and transport persisted.

From a contemporary vantage point, one can also observe that many of these methods have a tendency to be unhealthy. Either the method itself damages the food (for example, smoking produces carcinogens), or a significant number of unhealthy ingredients, such as salt and sugar, are added during the process. Many outdated techniques will fall short for those interested in food preservation for health reasons.

Napoleon Bonaparte sparked the search for a better technique of food preservation in the late 1700s. He was seeking a better way to feed his forces because he was of the opinion that "An army travels on its stomach." Napoleon thereupon promised a fortune to anyone who created a large-scale food preservation technique. Even though Nicholas Appert won the award in 1810, it was another 50 years before his approach reached the typical family. This happened soon after John Mason created the enduring "Mason Jar" in 1858.

Canning gained enormous popularity. It was a relatively easy process that was safe, efficient, and affordable. Now, practically anything can be preserved using a single technique.

The procedure of canning is really easy. First, food and fluids are placed in a glass jar or tin can (usually water). The container is heated and frequently put under pressure after being properly sealed. Any bacteria that could make people sick or ruin food are eliminated by this process. The air inside the can or jar contracts when it is taken out of the water, sealing the contents from the environment. The seal then shields the food from oxidation caused by air and new microbes entering. The food can then be easily preserved and consumed at a later time.

Almost every home continued to use canning until the advent of contemporary grocery stores. Both a need and a way of life, it was. Compare that to the present. In just a few generations, the vast majority of humanity has lost the ability to preserve food. However, over the past few years, there has been an increase in interest in food preservation, and canning, in particular, has become more and more popular.

Chapter 1: Understanding Canning & Preserving

Consider canning to be a type of cooking. A person is preparing food that they can keep and save rather than cooking just one meal to eat right away. Why should one do this? Because then a person can preserve the tastiest flavours at their prime for year-round enjoyment by canning! Imagine the incredible flavour of tomato sauce straight from the garden in the dead of winter.

By utilizing high temperatures to eliminate microbes and inactivate enzymes that could cause food to rot, the method of canning preserves fresh food in jars. As the jars cool, the vacuum seal that is created by the heating process seals them. Without oxygen, mould, yeast, and bacteria cannot thrive, preventing food from going bad.

The Two Canning Techniques: Pressure Canning and Water Bath Canning

One should either use the water-bath method or the pressure method to adequately and safely can and preserve their vegetables.

Which approach is best? This is based on how acidic the food is that a person is canning: Are they canning food with a high or low acid content? In other words, is the pH of the food high or low? The pH level of 4.6 serves as the dividing line between low-acid foods and high-acid foods; a pH higher than 4.6 indicates less acidity.

All a person needs to know is that high-acid foods can only be processed using water-bath canning, whereas low-acid foods must be processed using pressure canning. Low-acid environments are ideal for germs and toxins; therefore, one must use pressure canning to keep them from thriving. Security first!

1. Water Bath Canning

The less complicated of the two canning techniques is the water-bath method, which entails boiling the food in glass jars in a large pot of water. Boiling water canners, also known as water-bath canners, are pots with a large pot, a rack insert, and a lid that are specifically made for this purpose. But as long as one has a rack that fits within it and a top, any sizable, deep pot will suffice.

As a lower-temperature canning method (212°F), water-bath canning is only safe for high-acid vegetables and fruits. These foods' acidity, combined with the time spent in a boiling water bath, aids in their safe preservation without the need for high pressure. Pressure canning requires a larger investment, while water-bath canning is less complicated. It is referred to as "no pressure" canning.

2. Canning Under Pressure

When pressure canning, the temperature within the canner can reach 240°F, which is significantly greater than it could in a water-bath canner due to the tremendous pressure that is created when it is heated. Any hazardous bacteria, poisons, moulds, and yeasts are eliminated as a result.

To prevent the emergence of bacteria, particularly Clostridium botulinum, low-acid vegetables like corn and green beans MUST be cooked at a higher temperature—240°F at sea level. A beginner needs to spend money on a pressure canner that will do the job in order to keep the higher temperatures for the appropriate amount of time.

Low-acid items like meats, poultry, seafood, and chilli are also preserved using pressure canning, but they, too, require a higher temperature to boost the heat inside the jars above boiling for long enough to kill hazardous germs. Pressure canning may be enjoyable and rewarding, but one needs a "canner" to get started, and one must follow instructions—no improvising!

If a person wants to preserve low-acid foods but doesn't have access to a pressure canner, they might want to think about other methods of preservation. Broccoli, green beans and maize all taste much better when frozen and will have a superior texture when cooked according to an individuals preferred recipes. When freezing produce, it works best to blanch it briefly in boiling water, remove it, and quickly cool it off in ice water before draining and packing it into freezer bags or containers.

1.1 Basic Equipment to Start

In order to can food at home, there are a few basic supplies needed:

- Jars, lids, and screw bands for canning: Only use spotless jars free of nicks or cracks. Pressure canner or water-bath canner:

- If one has a pot with a fitted lid that is big enough to fully submerge the jars in water by 2 inches—and that will allow the water to boil when covered—they don't need to buy a specific water-bath canner for water-bath canning. A cake cooling rack will work as the inside-the-pot or inside-the-canner rack.

- Use only a pressure canner designed exclusively for, never a pressure cooker, when pressure canning.

- Jar lifter: Big "tongs" that make it easier to pick up hot jars, put them safely in a pot with boiling water, process them, and then remove them from the hot water.

- Ladle: Using a ladle makes loading food into canning jars easier.

- Wide-mouth canning funnels help one fill jars more easily and without spilling.

1.2 Where to Find Supplies for Canning

The majority of these canning necessities are available in kits that are sold on numerous websites, in hardware stores, craft stores, and other retail locations. These kits may also include other useful tools like magnetic lid lifters, plastic bubble removers, and jar scrubbers, headspace measuring tools—all the tools required to be successful.

Mason jars, screw-on lids, the water-bath canner can all be used repeatedly for many years, with the exception of single-use lids, which one must replace every year. These items are frequently available in good shape at yard sales, thrift shops, and in the basement of a friend or relative who has given up canning. One can definitely find a rack that suits their kettle in the neighbourhood hardware store, farm supply store, or online if they find a quality canner.

Each time one uses a jar, they should make sure to inspect it for any little chips or cracks, paying specific attention to the rim. It is advised to not try to use a rusty canner, either. People discover the hard way that rust areas may release leaks during processing, causing the gas burner's flame to flicker or go out completely and forcing me to quickly locate a different canning pot.

Chapter 2: The Fundamentals of Food Preservation

If a person wants to put everything into one sentence, then preservation may be summed up as an effort to stop growth. What is growing, if one may ask? Well, it's like this:

- Microorganisms

- Adverse enzymes

- Numerous chemical processes

- Confined and shielded from pests like rats and insects

It's not quite that simple, though, as certain preservation techniques actually depend on chemical processes or the development of specific bacteria. For example, several types of rice and cheese require the use of particular moulds, just as one would add yeast to some baking recipes. By triggering a chemical reaction in the cheese, these unique moulds can impart flavour and the proper textures.

The preservation of surplus produce is still another element and fundamental principle of food preservation and is, in fact, the entire justification for its existence. If a person were to rely only on their garden for food, they would undoubtedly need to cultivate an entire year's worth of food at once within the short growing season.

Obviously, this is an issue if there is no way to keep such objects safe. Canning and other food preservation techniques can be used in this situation. Once the gardening season is over, one has a year-round supply of food that won't go bad and leave them without food for the winter. However, there are other factors besides one's little garden that make maintenance so crucial. A beginner should examine the wider picture in the shape of global trade to do that. Everyone wants to have access to everything, and preservation makes it possible!

Back then, people were only allowed to plant things that could be grown in their territory and possibly in the surrounding regions. There was no possible method to transport tasty food from one continent to the other. Even travelling from one side of Europe to the other would have been a strenuous, scorching voyage. In the current world, food preservation has really made all of that possible.

2.1 Things to Consider for Beginners

It's critical to understand the food that an individual intends to can. Knowing if a meal is low or high-acid will help them decide whether to employ pressure canning or a water-bath method for preservation.

Botulism poisoning is the main worry. The botulinum toxin, which is created by the Clostridium bacteria, is what causes botulism, a disease. These bacteria are found in soil naturally and often do not pose a concern to humans. They do, however, live in low-acid, low-oxygen situations, such as those produced when one can get food, and are a very resilient form of bacteria. Food that has been inadequately canned becomes unsafe for ingestion as a result of the bacteria growing and producing their lethal toxin, botulin. By employing high heat (240° F) for low-acid foods or by utilizing high acidity to inactivate any toxins present, it is essential that the atmosphere inside the canned goods be unfriendly to the bacteria.

Following are some points to consider before canning,

- Use only the freshest, best-quality produce. Overripe fruits and vegetables should not be canned because they are on the verge of becoming bad!

- Make sure one has everything they need before they begin by gathering the supplies and ingredients. It's not time to dash to the store at this point in the procedure.

- Observe instructions and recipes in the letter. A person's family's safety depends on them executing things correctly, so don't improvise.

- When one is ready to fill the jars, sterilize them by washing them and then keeping them hot in a saucepan of boiling water. Without the boiling water pot, the task can easily be completed by using the dishwasher!

- When possible, use new lids, screw bands, and authentic canning jars. The sealing material in modern lids does not require heating before being applied to the jar top.

- Don't fill the jars all the way to the top. According to recipes, the "head space" can be either 1/4 inch or 1/2 inch. If an individual overfills the jars, the food may interfere with the sealant on the lid, preventing a tight closure.

- Before attaching the lid and screw band, it's crucial to clean the jar's rim and threads. Only finger tightening is used to tighten the band.

- Each jar should be placed on the rack in boiling water using the jar lifter. Bring the saucepan to a boil while making sure the jars are submerged in at least 1 to 2 inches of water. Once the water has reached a rolling boil once more, begin timing the procedure.

- Remove the lid and turn off the heat after the procedure is finished, releasing the steam away. With the help of the jar lifter, remove each jar and set it upright and a few inches apart on a towel to cool. Jars should cool for 12 to 24 hours.

- As the jars cool, they may hear a "popping" or "pinging" sound, which is one indication that the lids have sealed properly. Jars that don't seal should be used right away rather than being stored; instead, put them in the refrigerator.

- As long as they are kept in a cold, dry environment, the canned foods should generally remain fresh throughout the entire year. A damaged seal indicates that air has entered. Additionally, a bulging lid or one that appears corroded or rusty is a symptom of spoiling.

- If one ever opens a can and notices mildew, bubbles, or cloudiness, the seal has likely broken, and the contents are spoiled. They should not eat anything from it.

- Note that safe canning recommendations are constantly revised. For canning laws and other information, one can rely on the National Center for Home Food Preservation.

2.2 Benefits of Food Canning & Preserving

A person might want to be able to preserve fresh fruit or vegetables for as long as possible if they have a lot of seasonal leftovers from their garden that deteriorate too rapidly or if they have scored a particularly good deal at the grocery store. Whatever the circumstances are, here is an outline of all the advantages of home food preservation methods and why one should unquestionably learn how to perform them.

- **Always have an Abundance of Fresh Produce Close at Hand.**

No matter what a person decides to preserve or the method they use (canned goods, dried goods, frozen goods, or freeze-dried goods), one will always have an ample supply of the most delicious and fresh-tasting vegetables in their pantry or closet.

Aside from saving money, of course, anyone will admit that this is one of the best features of the whole process.

Making one's own preserves instead of purchasing them from a store will not only save a ton of money, but it will also turn out to be a much healthier option with much lower amounts of preservatives like sodium nitrite, sodium benzoate, and sulfur dioxide, which are frequently present in high concentrations in store-bought goods.

- **Being Perfectly Aware of the Ingredients**

It is so liberating to know what is in the food that someone is eating because they cooked it them self! One of the benefits is that a person has so much more control over the ingredients in their preserves, allowing them to concentrate more on living a healthy lifestyle rather than slogging through the internet, entering in ingredients with long names while trying to figure out what they all are. If one can't pronounce it, it's usually not good for them to eat; it is a general rule everyone should follow.

- **Being Aware of Food Security for Difficult Times.**

Occasionally, food costs increase in prices. The cost of food might swiftly and dramatically increase for reasons that are completely beyond a person's control.

Sometimes events on the other side of the world might have an impact on the quality of the food one buys at the store or even cause full shortages due to droughts or crops devastated by hailstorms. But none of that will be a concern for someone preserving food because they put a lot of time and effort into learning about the advantages of canning and preserving food as well as stocking up. The whole idea of food preservation is to save food while it is plentiful and consume it later. For example, the harvest season is when there are the most resources available for canning.

- **It's really practical!**

Imagine that it is Thanksgiving and that a person's entire family will be arriving in a few hours. But hold on, oh no! This is what? The cranberry sauce is gone! Don't worry, though; they've canned their produce, so they are ready for this kind of stuff. Instead of hurriedly rushing to the supermarket, battling long last-minute traffic jams, and squabbling over the last can of sauce, if any are still available! One can simply descend into the cellar and retrieve a can of the delicious cranberry sauce they cooked the previous year. In addition to being readily available, it is also secure and still tastes as good as the day they first sealed the jar.

- **The most crucial element, like any other, is that it's a pleasurable activity!**

There is nothing annoying about canning. The whole procedure is a lot of fun, and after the job is through, one truly does feel accomplished. It's mind-blowing how a person progresses from a seed to a garden to fruit. And that their hard work has paid off, and their closets are overflowing with the fruits of their effort. A person's entire family can participate in the canning and preservation

process, in addition to that. The wife can sterilize the jars; the son can pick the seeds that were planted earlier in the season. Everyone enjoys themselves, and when it's all said and done, one has a tasty, wholesome snack to enjoy after a hard day of being extraordinary!

However, there are other advantages to food canning and preservation as well.

- **Each bottle has the potential to be a gift for a friend, neighbour, or member of the family.**

Food canning and preservation can be nice housewarming presents for the neighbours who recently moved in or even a potential source of extra revenue if one wants to sell their hard work at the local farmer's markets and let the neighbourhood enjoy what the greatest darn beats this side of the state. Start food preservation, and canning is the basic lesson. It's a fun family activity that has the potential to earn some extra cash and will ensure one's family's security through trying times.

- **Benefits the Environment**

Canning food benefits the ecology by utilizing reusable mason jars rather than purchasing packaged goods in plastic, cardboard, or glass from the store. Naturally, if one reuses their lids multiple times, this is even more effective. This is one of the biggest invisible (unnoticed) benefits of food preservation that makes a person eco-friendlier and green.

- **One has a lot more options**

Not all stores are created equally, nor do they stock the same kinds of food. No human can picture a world if every shop sold everything. Seasonal varieties are not even mentioned in that.

Both of these won't be an issue for an individual if they are preserving their own food. Know why? since the pantry already contains everything! It doesn't matter if one purchased it from a store and canned it or if they cultivated it them self! They won't again have to worry about hopping between different supermarkets in search of those particular fruits and vegetables again because everything will be right there.

- **Less potentially dangerous chemicals consumption**

  When a person purchases processed goods, they eat a lot of highly unhealthy food. One's body is a sponge, soaking up everything one puts into it. A sponge floating in a sewage tank is hardly something one would want to use again. So why should one subject their body to that?

People should give themselves as many chances as possible to stay away from dangerous chemicals, and canning and dehydration are clearly the best ways to achieve that. A person is well aware of the contents of their possessions and can save their body the harmful substances. One of the greatest advantages of food preservation!

Start canning now!

Start little to prevent fatigue while canning at first. Beginners enjoy canning pickles. The majority of pickles just require 5 minutes of boiling water processing. One jar at a time, lift out the jars! To cool, spread them out on a hardwood tabletop or a cotton towel. It is the jars sealing if one hears popping noises. One should check the seal once the jars have cooled; the centre of the lid should be slightly pushed. Hence put an open jar in the refrigerator so one may eat it immediately soon. The labelled, sealed jars can be kept for the winter in the pantry.

Chapter 3: Water-Bath Canning

Making jams, jellies, and pickled vegetables through canning locks in the seasonal freshness of summer for year-round enjoyment. Anyone can safely keep food outside the refrigerator for up to a year by "water-bath canning," which involves heating jars in water. Boiling water baths or "Hot water canning" are other names for "Water-Bath Canning." It's one of two canning techniques (the other is pressure canning).

To safely can delicious food, one must understand how to properly sterilize jars, form the ideal seal, store the tasty canned products, and what to do if the jars don't seal. This chapter will guide one through every step of the entire canning procedure.

3.1 Why Water-Bath Canning?

Only food with a HIGH acid content should be canned in a water bath. Considering pickled veggies, tomatoes, berries, fruit, and sauerkraut. This suggests that water-bath canning is required when making jams and pickled vegetables. Because although users still need to be careful, the time they spend in a hot water bath and the fact that they are naturally acidic help to preserve them without the need for high pressure.

Canning foods in a water bath is not recommended if the internal temperature needs to be greater than the water's boiling point in order to destroy harmful microorganisms. These foods include meats, fish, poultry, chilli and beans, corn, and other low-acid vegetables. Foods that are low in acid must be canned under pressure.

What Equipment Is Required for Canning?

To get started, a beginner will need to put together some equipment. Although there are several ways to reduce costs, food safety considerations should guide all of the decisions.

A huge, deep pot constructed typically of aluminium is called a boiling water canner. It is so deep that it completely submerges the jars and have fitting lids. The greatest bottoms are flat (to work on all cooktops).

In order to keep the jars elevated above the direct heat at the bottom of the stockpot, a rack is also needed. Jars will crack from the heat if they are placed directly on the bottom of the canner.

Wide-mouth and narrow-mouth varieties of canning jars are available in a variety of sizes, ranging from four ounces to half pints, pints, quarts, and quarts. The jars can always be used again.

Bands made of metal that are undamaged, rust-free, and suit all jars. These hold the lids in place while the items are being processed by screwing them onto the threaded jar rims. Cooled and sealed. If the bands are not dented or broken, one can reuse them.

Metal canning lids that are single-use and fit the jars. Every time a beginner process food, brand-new lids are required. During processing (heating in the canner), the inner gasket in these lids softens, allowing air to escape from the jar during chilling and solidifying an airtight seal as the jars cool.

A funnel for canning. This wide-mouthed funnel, which is best made of plastic or stainless steel, prevents food from spilling onto the jar's rim as one fills it.

A ladle made of steel. If someone is purchasing a new one, choose a long-handled type with a pouring spout or rim.

A jar raiser These specialised tongs fit around the base of the canning jar rims and are used to either lower hot jars into a canner filled with boiling water or properly grasp and raise hot jars straight up out of the canner after processing.

Food processor or strainer. These appliances, which come in a variety of shapes and sizes, are made for blending soft, cooked foods and screening them to separate the pulp from the skins and seal. It is still preferred to use by many the vintage, hand-cranked Food Mill.

A stainless steel stockpot is big enough to accommodate and prepare a significant quantity of tomatoes, berries, or other goods before one ladles them into the canning jars for canner processing.

Utilize the Proper Cooking Surface.

Use a gas or electric burner to can food in a water bath. No matter what one may have heard or how nice it may sound, canning in an oven, microwave, or dishwasher is not safe. Additionally, it is unsafe to can tomatoes and fruit items by simply boiling the jars and lids to sterilise them before filling the jars with a hot product and sealing them with a lid and screw band. The contents of the jars have not been heated sufficiently to prevent the growth of bacteria, toxins, moulds, or yeast while the jars are stored at room temperature, even though the seals on the jars are strong and keep their seal.

The U.S. Department of Agriculture (USDA) claims that research warns that ALL of these appliances are NOT SAFE for home canning, even for high-acid foods, despite the fact that some of the new multi-cookers have a canning capability.

Another issue that affects home canners is smooth glass stovetops. Some water-bath canner designs feature recessed bottoms that make it difficult for heat from the glass top to be evenly dispersed during processing. Additionally, a significant amount of heat may be reflected back to the glass from the canner, overheating it. This could result in the glass breaking or turning on the burner's shut-off feature, underprocessing the canner load. The USDA advises following the recommendations of one's stove manufacturer if they have a smooth, glass cooking surface since "styles of smooth cooktops being made differ in ways that influence appropriateness for canning."

3.2 A Step-by-Step Guide to Water-Bath Canning

Here is how one can preserve using a water bath step-by-step.

An amateur should get started by having their supplies and produce ready in advance. All jars, their lids, and their bands need to be cleaned in a dishwasher or with hot water and soap.. Check the fit of the bands. The jars' rims and bodies should also be free of any dents or cracks. The lids should always be brand-new.

Step 1: The jars must be heated before being filled with hot contents and placed in a hot canner. The clean jars need to be put in a large, separate saucepan and not the canner, completely submerged in water, and the water needs to be brought to a boil for 10 minutes.

Step 2: Separately preheat the water-bath canning pot. When halfway full, add water. Set the temperature of the water to simmer at 180°F. If one has a canning pot, hang the jar rack within it. Keep the water simmering on the stovetop until Step 8 below, when one has filled each jar with the prepared food and immediately placed the jars into the canner.

Step 3: Remove and dry the jars. Then, while the jars are still warm, fill them with the prepared mixture. A wide funnel is used to ladle the food into the jar.

Step 4: To get rid of any air bubbles that may have been trapped, gently stir the contents of the jar with a cleaned spatula.

Step 5: Wipe the jar rims well with a damp towel to remove any food residue. Before the band is applied, each jar needs to have a lid on it. Screws in jars should be finger-tight but not too tight.

Step 6: Using the jar lifter, place sealed jars on the canner's rack. Don't let the jars come in contact. Jars must be immersed in liquid, ideally at a depth of 1 to 2 inches. Use hot water from a separate kettle if you need more hot water.

Step 7: Turn up the heat until the canner's water boils. Set the timer once the water starts to boil. Even though each recipe is different, it is usual to boil the entire jars for about 10 minutes.

Step 8: After everything has been completed, turn off the heat and lift the canner's lid to allow the steam to escape. For five to ten minutes, jars should cool in the canner.

Step 9: Remove the jars from the canner using the jar lifter, then spread them out on a surface like a cloth or a rack. As the jars cool, one should hear them "ping," signifying that they have successfully sealed.

Jars should be left to cool for 12 to 24 hours in step 10. Don't tighten bands again in order to avoid compromising the seam's ability to seal.

Step 11: After the jars have completely cooled, check the seals once more, gently press the centre of each lid. The jar is properly sealed if there is no give. The lid does not seal if it recoils. After placing the jar in the refrigerator, consume within two weeks.

Containers should be kept in a cold, dry, and dark place for up to a year, according to the National Center for Home Food Preservation. When one opens the jar, if anything seems odd or smells weird, or if the lid is broken, one should not eat it.

Chapter 4: Easy Water-Bath Recipes for Beginners

Canning is a great old skill that is coming back in a big way. Anyone can preserve delectable food using ingredients from the grocery store or their own garden with the help of these simple water bath canning recipes for beginners! An individual need to D these recipes if they've never canned before! It's thrilling and terrifying all at once when one first decides to start canning! A beginner might already have a plan for what to can initially, but they might also just love the concept of canning their own food in general and need a starting point.

Before moving on to more difficult recipes and methods, these water bath canning recipes will give the perfect first taste (pun intended) of canning. They are simple to make and even simpler to preserve.

4.1 Classic Dill Pickles with Garlic

A traditional dill and garlic pickle recipe. Processing in a hot water bath is necessary for shelf storage. All the jars can be kept in the refrigerator for up to six weeks if a novice wants to omit the hot water bath. This dish makes four-pint jars (500 mL). Simply process the mixture for a longer period of time if one wants to produce two quart- or litre-sized jars. The time taken does not include the amount of time needed to heat water for the jars and put them back to a simmer once they have been filled. Add 15 to 30 minutes.

Prep Time: 24 minutes

Cook Time: 5 minutes

Servings: 4-5

Ingredients

- Tiny pickled cucumbers, 3–4 pounds

- Vinegar, two cups

- 2-cups of water

- 2/TBS pickling salt

- 8 dill heads

- 8 peeled garlic cloves

- 2 teaspoons mustard seeds

- 1 teaspoon peppercorns

- Optional: 1/2 tsp spicy pepper flakes

Instructions

Get Cucumbers Ready

Step 1: With a gentle brush, wash and lightly scrub.

Step 2: To assist stop blossom ends from softening, slice them thinly. Long and wide cucumbers should be cut into quarters lengthwise to fit in jars.

Step 3: Place in the ice water bath for up to 8 hours while preparing the rest.

Prepare the Canner and Jars.

Step 4: Water should be added to a big pot or canner until the jars are covered by 1 inch of water.

Step 5: Before placing them in the canner, inspect the jars for cracks and wash them in warm, soapy water.

Step 6: Heats the jars (no need to sterilise as final processing will be longer than 10 minutes).

Make Brine.

Step 7: Combine vinegar, water, and pickling salt in a medium pot. Salt will dissolve after five minutes of simmering after bringing to a boil.

Filled jars

Step 8: Empty the hot jars from the canner.

Step 9: Each pint jar should contain 2 dill sprigs, 2 garlic cloves, 1/2 tsp mustard seeds, 1/4 tsp peppercorns, and 1/8 tsp hot pepper flakes (double if using quart jars). Cucumbers should be packed into jars to within 3/4 inch of the rim.

Step 10: Cover the cucumbers with a hot vinegar brine. Remove any air bubbles with a plastic utensil before adding more brine, allowing a 1/2 inch headspace.

Step 11: Cleanly wipe the rim, then use a hot-sealing lid to seal it. The band is screwed on; then, it is finger-tightened.

Step 12: For quart (1 L) jars, a process in a hot water bath for 15 minutes as opposed to 10 minutes for pint (500 mL) jars.

Step 13: Makes 2 quart (1.5 L) or 4 pints (500 mL) jars.

Step 14: National Center for Home Food Preservation processing time. If one is cooking at an altitude greater than 1000 feet (306 metres) above sea level, remember to modify the cooking times.

Notes

Before consuming, give pickles four weeks to mellow. The pickle jars that have been heated and sealed will last for many years, but for the greatest flavour and texture, use them within a year. Once opened, keep in the refrigerator for up to a year.

Optional: To reduce the acidity of the vinegar without making them into sweet pickles, add 2 to 3 Tablespoons of sugar to the brine along with the salt.

4.2 Apple Butter

Is Apple butter preserved by water bath canning? Anyone can prepare canned goods using this very basic, safety-tested recipe. Cooked-down, caramelized apple sauce is known as apple butter. Everyone adores eating apple butter on toast because it is so good. Making apple butter is fun for beginners when because making it is so easy. Let's get started!

Prep Time: 30 minutes

Cook Time: 1 hour

Servings: 3-4

Equipment

- Cutting board

- Knife

- Slicer, Corer Peeler.

- Either a large stainless steel pot or a Dutch oven that has been enameled

- Weighing cups

- Ladle or Food Processor or Food Mill

- Water-Bath Canner

Ingredients

- Pint or 1/2 Pint Size canned goods

- Wide-mouth or standard canning lids (depending on what jars one is using)

- Wide mouth or standard canning rings (depending on what jars one is using)

- Bottle Lifter/De-bubbler

- Measurer of headspace

- Funnel

Instructions

Step 1: With warm, soapy water, wash the jars and lids. Make sure there are no chips or bubbles in the glass of the jars.

Step 2: Use cold water to wash the apples. Apples should be peeled, cored, and chopped. One may enjoy using the apple slicer, corer, and peeler. It facilitates a quick and simple process. A vegetable peeler, knife, and chopping board can also be used to complete the process. In order to preserve more colour and flavour, one can leave the skins on while making this recipe.

Step 3: In a Dutch oven made of enamel or stainless steel, add the apples. Over high heat, bring the apples to a boil. Apples should be simmered for a long period of time, covered, on low heat.

Step 4: When the apples are soft, remove them from the fire and let them cool somewhat. The apples should be processed in batches till it's smooth.

Step 5: In the stainless steel or Dutch oven with enamel, add the apple purée once more. Add the ground cinnamon, apple cider, and 1 cup of brown sugar. The brown sugar should be gradually increased to two cups of sugar after tasting it. If necessary, add extra ground cinnamon.

Step 6: Cook the apple mixture, often stirring, at a gentle boil over medium heat until it thickens and retains its shape. Scooping a tiny amount of food onto a plate will allow one to test it. An individual should reduce sufficiently to make apple butter if the liquid and apples don't separate.

Step 7: In the process of boiling down the apple mixture. The water bath canner should be on the burner. The water bath canner should now contain the canning rack. The pint or 1/2 pint jars should be added to the water bath canner. As one heats the water, it will begin to warm. Add enough water to at least 2-3 inches over the jars' tops. The jars should cook for 10 minutes after being brought to a boil.

Step 8: Using the jar lifter, remove the jars one at a time from the water bath canner. To make sure there is still 2-3 inches of water over the jars, pour water from the jar into the water bath canner. Pour a ladleful of the hot mixture into the jar leaving some space.

Step 9: Make sure to eliminate all air bubbles with the de-bubbler. One should repeat this process several times to get rid of as many air bubbles as one can because apple butter has a thicker consistency, and they can be hidden. If required, adjust the headspace by adding more hot apple butter.

Step 10: To make sure the lid forms a tight seal, wipe the jar's rim. Place the band around the jar's fingertip and centre the lid. Using the jar lifter, place the jar back into the water bath canner.

Step 11: Up until the jars are full, repeat steps 8 through 10 with the leftover apple butter.

Step 12: The water bath canner rack should be lowered into the boiling water. Make sure there are at least 2 inches of water in the jars. Start the processing time when the water is boiling; if the water is not yet boiling. For 10 minutes, process pint and 1/2 pint jars. A time adjustment for altitude should always be made. To ensure that one is processing for the appropriate time, set a timer. Turn off the heat and take the canner lid off when the timer goes off. Give the jars five minutes in the water.

Step 13: Out of the water, raise the canning rack. Carefully transfer the jars to a wire rack or kitchen towel to cool using the jar lifer. One should t ry to avoid tilting the jars when transporting them because doing so could affect the seal. Before handling, let the jars cool for 12 to 24 hours.

Step 14: Remove the canning rings from the jars once they have cooled. To make sure there is no food residue left over from processing on the outside of the jars, wash them clean. Put the recipe name and the date on the jar's label. The date will enable one to use the oldest canned items first and will help recall the recipe one used to can.

4.3 Cranberry Sauce

Prep Time: 10 minutes

Cook Time: 10 minutes

Servings: 1-2

Equipment

- Canner

- Jars for canning

- Container lids

- Ring canning

- French oven

- Rubber spatula

- Funnel

- Ladle

- Clean towels

Ingredients:

- Orange juice, 1 cup and orange zest 1tsp

- 50 g of sugar

- 12 ounces of cranberries

Instructions

Step 1: Fill the water in the water bath canner to get it ready. Once the water is boiling, all one needs it to have enough water to cover the jars by 2 inches.

Step 2: On the stove, place the canner. Activate the burner on high.

Step 3: Clean and disinfect the jars. To prevent them from cracking when put in the canner, one should keep them warm. They can be baked on a tray at 170 degrees F or filled with hot water.

Step 4: Put the cleaned lids in a fresh bowl and set them aside.

Step 5: Combine orange juice and sugar in a medium pot, up to a boil.

Step 6: Turn down the heat to medium, afterward bowl and mix in the cranberries. Let it simmer until one sees the cherries pop.

Step 7: Smash the cranberries with a potato masher until they are the appropriate texture.

Step 8: Spend the next 10 minutes constantly stirring the mixture.

Step 9: Add the orange zest after removing it from the heat.

Step 10: Fill the jars with the warm cranberry sauce, leaving a headspace of half an inch. Get rid of any bubbles in the container.

Step 11: To make sure the jar rim is free of any food, wipe it down with a clean, moist cloth.

Step 12: Put a spotless lid on the container. Tighten to the tip of the finger, then add a ring.

Step 13: Place the jars in the boiling water using canning tongs. Once the water is back at a rolling boil, cover the canner and process for 15 minutes.

Step 14: Remove the lid, turn off the heat, and let the canner set for five minutes after the 15 minutes are up.

Step 15: Place the jars on a thick towel in a location where they won't be disturbed for 12 hours after removing them with the canning tongs.

Step 16: By pressing down in the centre of the lid after 12 hours, examine the seal on the jars. If there is any give, either reprocess or refrigerate and use those jars within the following month. For 12 to 18 months, keep in a cold, dark location.

4.4 Crushed Tomatoes

Prep Time: 2 minutes

Cook Time: 1 hour 20 minutes

Servings: 8-12

Ingredients

- 6 kg of tomatoes (approximately to fill a quart jar)

- 4 teaspoons of lemon juice in a bottle (per quart jar)

- 2 spoons of salt (per quart jar)

- 2 spoons of sugar (per quart jar)

Instructions

Step 1: After 30 to 60 seconds in boiling water, immerse tomatoes into the icy water. The task is made simpler if one boils water in one huge kettle, puts the tomatoes in another large kettle, and then pours the hot water over them. After letting the tomatoes stand for two minutes, rinse them and put them in the cold water bath.

Step 2: Peel the skins after removing the core.

Step 3: Slice into fourths.

Step 4: Some of the quartered tomatoes should be placed in a big kettle, mashed with a potato masher, and heated quickly.

Step 5: Continue stirring and gradually add the remaining quartered tomatoes. Boil gently for 5 minutes after adding all the tomatoes.

Step 6: Tomatoes should be packed into hot, clean quart-sized canning jars, leaving 1/2-inch headspace.

Step 7: To each quart jar, add 2 tablespoons of lemon juice and 1 teaspoon each of salt and sugar. By moving a spatula or bubble freer between the tomatoes and the jar's side, one can release extra air from the jar.

Step 8: Use suitably prepared lids to clean the rims and caps of the jars. In a boiling water canner, process the bands for 50 minutes after screwing them on.

4.5 Chili Zucchini Marmalade

Prep Time: 30 minutes

Cook Time: 2 hours 30 minutes

Servings: 8-10

Ingredients

- 3 oranges

- 2 lemons

- gingerroot chunk, sliced to be an inch thick

- 4 shredded zucchini measured in cups (peeled and seeds removed)

- 2 apples, peeled, cored, and chopped.

- 5 cups sugar

- 2 ghost chilli peppers, fresh and minced (wear gloves, it's hot!)

- 2 -4 blossoms of calendula, which can be used for colouring but are optional (optional), or two to four drops of yellow food colouring (optional)

Instructions

Step 1: Use a vegetable peeler to remove the orange zest, then slice it very thinly and set it in a large saucepan made of stainless steel with a hefty bottom.

Step 2: Oranges should have the white pith removed, and lemons should have the peel and pith removed. Wrap the ginger root in cheesecloth and place it in the container. Wrap the cloth in a knot, then place it in the pot.

Step 3: While standing over the pot, cut the oranges and lemons so that the segments fall into the pot. Discard the membrane and seeds after slicing the segments. Attempting to extract as much juice as possible into the saucepan.

Step 4: To complete the recipe, add the remaining components to the saucepan.

Step 5: Sugar should be dissolved as the mixture is brought to a boil over medium-high heat. Raise the temperature to be high, bring the mixture to a boil, and continue to stir it often until it reaches the gelatinous stage. It can take up to an hour to finish. To extract all of the flavours from the mixture into the marmalade, place the spice bag in a strainer and give it a thorough squeeze. Put the bag in the trash. Take off the foam.

Step 6: In the meantime, get the water bath ready and get the jars and lids ready for the canning process.

Step 7: Place the marmalade in the jars, allowing a head space of about a quarter of an inch. Get rid of any air bubbles. After wiping the rims, replace the lids. Put on the bands so that they are fingertip tight.

Step 8: Put the cover on and then place the dish in a water bath that is boiling. Perform the operation for ten minutes. Take off the lid of the saucepan, then turn off the heat. Let sit for 5 minutes. Transfer to a location free of draughts.

Step 8: Label and put away. Make use of it during the next year.

4.6 Pickled Green Beans

Prep Time: 10 minutes

Cook Time: 10 minutes

Servings: 4-5

Ingredients

- 2 1/2 cups of white vinegar, distilled

- 2 and a half cups of mild, not hard, water

- 14 cup salt for pickling

- 2 1/2 to 3 pounds of freshly cut, cleaned green beans

- 3 garlic cloves

- 1 fresh dill bunch

- 4-6 Thai peppers

Instructions

Step 1: Bring vinegar, water, and salt to a boil in a medium saucepan. Stirring and boiling are used to dissolve the salt. Keep warm in a low heat setting.

Step 2: Boiling three quart-sized canning jars in a big saucepan of boiling water will sterilize the jars, lids, and rings. Green beans, a sprig of dill, and one or two Thai chilis should be packed snugly into the jars while leaving the lids and rings in the water so that the jars keep warm and move rapidly.

Step 3: Pour the vinegar mixture over the green beans until it is just a quarter-inch from the lip. Clean the rims, place a lid on top, and then snugly screw on the rings.

Step 4: For ten minutes, process the jars in a hot water bath (15 minutes for above 6,000 feet altitude). Put the jars on a fresh, dry towel after removal. Verify that no one is touching. Let it cool.

Step 5: As they cool, the jars will pop and seal. Any open jars can be put in the refrigerator and used right away.

4.7: Sweet and Sour Gherkins

Prep Time: 10 minutes

Cook Time: 35 minutes

Servings: 6 (1-litre) jars

Ingredients:

- 4.5 kilograms of fresh gherkins.

- 500g of sea salt, fine.

- White spirit vinegar in 0.8 litres.

- White mustard seed, 6 tsp. Per jar, 1 tsp.

- Coriander seed, 6 teaspoons. Per jar, 1 tsp.

- 1 1/2 teaspoons of black peppercorns Per jar, 1/4 tsp.

- 6 fresh peppers de chile (optional). Per jar, one pepper.

- Twelve new garlic gloves. Two cloves in each jar.

- A lot of new dills, flower heads, stalks, and leaves.

Instructions

Getting the Gherkins ready

Step 1: Cleanse the cucumbers well in cold water, then trim the blossom ends' petals. Step 2: Throw away any cucumbers that appear sad. Any bruising or damaged skin should be removed. Get rid of any stems that are left.

Step 3: Remove 1-2 mm of the cucumber's tip at the blossom end using a sharp knife. By eliminating the pectinase-producing microorganisms from the blossom end, one can prevent pectinase from degrading the pectin in the cucumbers and resulting in softness.

Brine the Gherkins in Salt

Step 4: The cucumbers will be brined in a salt solution as the next phase. One shall utilise a 10% brine in this situation. Osmosis will draw water from the gherkins, enhancing their crispness in the final product.

Step 5: Then add 500g of fine sea salt to 5 litres of lukewarm water in a large, non-metallic bowl or food-safe plastic bucket. The salt must be well mixed until it dissolves.

Step 6: Add the cucumbers after the water has cooled.

Step 7: Allow to stand for about 12 hours or overnight. Then the gherkins should be taken out and washed in cold water.

Gherkins' packaging and canning

With the exception of the additional steps below, use the conventional procedures for water bath canning. It is strongly advised to read the USDA Complete Guide to Home Canning if someone is new to canning. The National Center for Home Food Preservation website offers a free download of it.

It's interesting that this canning recipe calls for keeping the gherkin jars in a water bath with a temperature of less than 1000C. Keep the temperature here between 82°C and 85°C. It is considerably simpler than it might sound and needs the use of a thermometer. To preserve the gherkins' crisp texture, the procedure, which might be described as low-temperature pasteurisation, is required. The pectin content of cucumbers begins to break down at temperatures exceeding 85 °C, softening them.

Step 8: Heat the water in the water bath canner to about 60 C after filling it halfway.

Step 9: Put a pan with the vinegar mixture and water over medium heat. Stir in the sugar until it is completely dissolved. The brine should be heated to a temperature of about 85 °C.

Step 10: Gherkins should be packed snugly into the sterilised jar. As one go, add the spices, garlic, and dill. Cut some of the gherkins shorter if necessary to fit.

Step 11: After removing any air bubbles, pour the hot vinegar solution into the jars. Place the sterilised jars in the canner after attaching the lids.

Step 12: To cover the jars by at least 2 cm, pour more boiling water from a kettle.

Step 13: Increase the canner's temperature to 82°C on high heat, then reduce the heat to maintain the range of 82–85°C for 30 minutes. One must keep a tight eye on the thermometer; if it overheats, just add some ice water to bring the temperature down.

Step 14: After 30 minutes, turn off the heat, remove the jars from the canner, and let them sit there for 5 minutes before taking them out and laying them away to cool.

Gherkin Storage & Serving

The gherkins will be edible in about 3 weeks. Gherkins lose their crisp texture over time in their jars; according to experience, they should be eaten within 18 months. Once opened, store the jars in the refrigerator and use them within two to three weeks.

Chapter 5: Pressure Canning

Even for beginners, pressure canning can be frightening, but it's well worth it. A beginner should not just use a water bath can jam and pickles! Low-acid foods like vegetables, soups, and meat can all be securely canned if one understands how to use a pressure canner.

Pressure canning is frightening, to begin with. Even if someone has done water bath canning for years, they can still feel anxious when they run their first batch in the pressure canner. The following questions can occur; Is this device secure? Did I do it correctly? Am I going to set my kitchen on fire?

How does Pressure Canning Work?

A pressure canner successfully heats and processes low acid items, including meat, vegetables, beans, and soups, by applying pressure to produce temperatures considerably above boiling. Jams, pickles, and other high acid foods (pH ≤ 4.6) can be preserved with a boiling water bath canner, although low acid foods may contain more virulent microorganisms.

Most people still recall from high school physics that, at least at sea level, water boils at 212 degrees Fahrenheit (100 degrees Celsius). Due to decreased pressure at higher altitudes, water boils at lower temperatures at higher elevations, dropping by 1 degree F for every 500 feet in elevation gain. In contrast, a pressure canner raises boiling temperatures by increasing pressure.

The majority of food is processed at 10 pounds of pressure, or 240 degrees Fahrenheit, at sea level. For the same result at high altitudes, greater pressure is required.

Low acid foods are shelf stable and can be kept for a long time on the pantry shelf when properly processed and sealed in a pressure canner.

What Foods Need to be Pressure Canned?

Not all foods require canning under pressure. Low acid items, such as vegetables, soups, and meats, are the only ones that necessitate the higher sterilizing temperatures inside a pressure canner.

Peaches and apples are examples of high acid fruits (pH ≤ 4.6) that only require minimal processing in a water bath canner. The same is true for pickles, which are made acidic by adding vinegar. Pressure canners are required for low-acid meat and seafood, stews, and veggies.

This comprises:

- The meat of All Sorts, including Beef, Chicken, and Pork

- Both meat and vegetable stocks and broths

- Potatoes, pumpkin, green beans, and other vegetables

- Dry beans, such as pinto, navy, and black beans.

- Boiled beans and chilli

- Stews and soups

- Some tomato-based products, such as spaghetti sauce, contain low-acid components, including peppers, onions, and mushrooms.

Foods that can't be Canned Under Pressure

Even in a pressure canner, not everything can be safely preserved by canning. Regardless of the technique, the following foods cannot be safely canned at home:

- Butter, milk, and other dairy products

- Coconut Milk

- Corn starch, most thickeners, and flour

- Pasta, rice, and other carbohydrates

- Pickled eggs

- Eggs

There are some items that just don't do well at pressure canning temperatures, in addition to those that cannot be preserved using any canning technique.

Is Pressure Canning Really Required?

A pressure canner is not mentioned in extremely ancient canning manuals from the first decade of the 20th century. Meat and veg with a low acidity need extended processing times, sometimes up to 5 hours, in a simple water bath canner.

Although it did prevent the food from "spoiling" in the jar, the risk of botulism was still present. If the pH is higher than 4.6, botulism spores can survive in a boiling water bath canner and then start to grow inside the sealed jars.

Its growth is inhibited by the strong acidity (low pH) of fruits and pickles, but it can flourish in water-bath-canned meats and vegetables.

First, there has to be any possibility of botulism. Its spores are prevalent in the soil and surroundings, but whether they end up inside the canning jar is essentially just a question of chance. They cannot develop if they are absent. Although the spores can potentially be found anywhere, the risk is greatest with root vegetables and other items in contact with the ground. Similar to playing Russian roulette, the chances are slim, but the results could be disastrous.

Second, granny was aware that items with low acid content that she had water bath canned required a minimum 10-minute boil. While boiling does not eliminate botulism spores during canning, if the toxin was created inside the canned product, it is denatured. So she removed those green beans from the water bath canning after 3+ hours and cooked them on high heat for at least 10 minutes.

Third, to prevent food from rotting, canned items were frequently kept in the cold cellar rather than on a shelf in the pantry that was kept at room temperature on grandma's day. A cold cellar and canning worked together to sterilize and reduce risks by preventing problems.

Vegetables and meats can still be preserved using the water bath method, which requires 3 to 5 hours of canner maintenance. They now understand that in order to lower the hazards, the meals must be boiled at a high temperature for at least 10 minutes.

Additionally, a product of far higher quality is produced. It is actually much friendlier to heat the foods to a high temperature (about 240 F in the canner) for a brief period than to water bath can them for a long time, then boil them on the stove without the jar.

What does a person suppose will be left of those green beans after they've canned them for three hours, drained them, and boiled them for an additional ten minutes? The response is a slimy muddle. Instead, one should use a pressure can; it's considerably more dependable, safe, and genuinely simple once one figures out how. Nowadays, mostly people actually prefer pressure canning to water bath canning because it is quicker and generates significantly less heat in the kitchen. Results are comparable to water bath canning and occasionally much better.

Types of Pressure Canners

Dial gauge and weighted gauge pressure canners are the two primary types. They function somewhat differently, and the majority of recipes for pressure canning actually include two separate sets of instructions or processing pressures, one for each type.

Weighted Gauge Pressure Canner

With a weight on the steam valve, this sort of pressure canner is "set," often to 5, 10, or 15 PSI. The weight jiggles, and some steam is released when the canner reaches that temperature. Since they are typically sold under regulation, these are simpler to handle

Once the weight reaches the desired temperature, one reduces the heat such that it jiggles once every minute or so. By doing this, an individual can be confident that the canner will remain hot enough to safely prepare the food while not continually releasing steam. That corresponds to low to medium heat on the stove.

They are simple to use because one doesn't need to constantly watch over this kind of canner, and it will consistently sustain pressure without needing modifications. The only three available settings are at 5, 10, or 15 PSI, which is a drawback.

If someone is below 1000 feet in elevation, most foods are processed at 10 PSI. To ensure that safe temperatures are reached beyond 1000 feet, the only choice is to increase the pressure to 15 PSI.

On the other hand, one may move up to 12 PSI at an elevation of slightly over 1000 feet (instead of jumping to 15).

Dial Gauge Pressure Canner

When using a dial gauge canner, pressure is controlled by keeping an eye on the dial at the top. One must be present to control the heat as the canner processes the food so that the pressure always remains above the desired level. It costs one time and attention, but it enables a beginner to maintain an intermediate temperature (for instance, 12 PSI).

When using a dial gauge, a person monitors the canner by ear, listening to make sure it "jiggles" around once every minute. With the hands, one may quickly complete other tasks and efficiently utilize the time.

How to Use a Pressure Canner

Once an individual has completed the process a few times, they won't need to refer to the instructions because the procedure is actually rather straightforward. One should start by reading the directions in their canner's manual because they can differ slightly from one another.

Following are the instruction on how to operate a weighted gauge pressure canner. The instructions may differ whether someone has a dial gauge or a different brand, but the fundamental steps will generally be very similar.

Prep for Pressure Canning

There are a few things one should do to make sure the canner is in good operating order before beginning the first batch.

Make sure that the seals and gaskets appear to be in good condition. For a gasket-less canner to seal well, the metal-on-metal contact point is frequently lubricated with a tiny drop of olive oil. Before one begins, put a little olive oil on the finger and rub it along the seal.

Find all the components! This contains the canner, the canner lid, the canning weight, and the canning trivet (or trivets for double-layer canners). Although it may sound foolish, one may regret loading the canner before looking for the canning weight. It is pretty distressing when the canner is hot, and none can find the canning weight.

Prepare Food for Pressure Canning

This will be a recipe-specific discussion. Some raw pack recipes only require one to pack the food into the jars, add boiling water to the top, and place them in the canner. Others call for pre-cooking or blanching the food in order to maintain texture or stop raw food from clumping together during the canning process. A beginner should use a tried-and-true canning recipe and adhere to the given directions.

Pre Heating the Pressure Canner

A pressure canner is not entirely submerged in water, in contrast to water bath canning. A person needs enough water to both fill the chamber with pressurized steam and keep the canner from running out of water while the procedure is taking place. One should always read the directions because canner models differ. Most call for beginners to first add 2 to 3 inches of water to the bottom. After that, one should add the bottom canning trivet. It stops the jars from coming into direct contact with the canner's heated bottom, which could lead to thermal shock and cause the jars to break.

Now one can start the canner's pre-heating process, but a beginner should always avoid bringing it to a full rolling boil. That is crucial!

The water in the canner should be quite hot for raw pack recipes, just hot enough to burn one's hand (around 140 F). The canner water should be just simmering for hot pack recipes (around 180 F). These temperatures aid in ensuring that the food entering the canner is at a temperature that is roughly equivalent to that of the canner. Jars could break from thermal shock if the canner is significantly hotter or colder than the contents of the jars.

A beginner does not need to get out a thermometer and worry too much about it because there is a reasonable amount of room for error in this situation. But there's still a 30% risk that learners might break the jar if they put a raw packed jar full of room temperature food into a boiling canner. It's better for an individual to try their best to keep the temps at simmering (180 F) for hot packs and pretty darn hot (140 F) for raw packs.

Loading Pressure Canner

When a starter is finishing up food preparation and packing it into canning jars while the pressure canner is heating up, they should be mindful of headspace and use the amount of headspace called for in the recipe.

With two-part canning lids, a beginner should make sure the jars are finger-tight (or as tight as one can turn the lids with just their fingertips, rather than fully cranked down on there). It shouldn't be too loose that the contents leak into the canner, but it should be loose enough that air can escape helping generate a vacuum as the jars cool. Again, there's a pretty wide margin for error here, so one should take no sweat too much. Contents leaking, also known as siphoning, indicates that those jars are too loose or that the headspace is too tiny. Jar lids buckling indicates that they are tightened too much.

As a person prepares the jars to keep them warm, they should place them inside the canner (on top of the bottom trivet). If their canner has two layers, they should place the spacer trivet between them and continue stacking jars until they run out of room or their canner is filled. The jars should ideally be slightly offset so that they are not piled squarely on top of the lower jars. This should improve the canner's internal steam circulation.

Pressure Canner Seal Closing Techniques

Depending on the model, pressure canners can be sealed. Most manufacturers' bolts just turn and click into place. One should pay attention to the directions on the canner.

No matter what kind of canner one uses, make sure one has prepared the seal by either inspecting the gasket twice before proceeding or, in the case of canners without gaskets, by lubricating the contact points. Before one seals it, one should make sure the lid is sufficiently straight.

Opening a Steam Pressure Canner

A beginner by now has secured the lid, but the canner isn't yet "sealed" in the traditional sense, and pressure hasn't yet built up. For that, turn the heat up to its highest setting and open the steam vent while bringing the canner to a boil. One cannot just close the steam vent before the canner is filled with steam for the food to process properly.

Before adding the canning weight (weighted gauge) or shutting the steam vent, one should give the canner a full 10 minutes to vent steam (dial gauge). This guarantees that the canner's contents are all at a boil and that the steam-filled chamber is completely filled. Skipping this step may result in incorrect food processing and cool pockets inside the canner. When a constant stream of steam emerges from the vent, not before, begin timing the venting. When using a raw pack, the canner may not even start to steam for 10 to 15 minutes as the contents heat up. After that, one must wait a further ten minutes to allow steam to escape before sealing the vent.

Pressure Canner Steam Venting

After that, it's time to completely seal the canner and bring it up to pressure when the steam has vented for the entire 10 minutes. This is accomplished using a weighted gauge by placing the canning weight on the steam vent. It has three sides, and depending on the amount of pressure one needs to use inside the canner; one must select the side with the label. The altitude and the recipe are factors in this.

Processing Food in a Pressure Canner

The canner will take anywhere from 10 to 40 minutes to reach pressure. One should not start timing when sealing the canner because this is not included in the "process time" in the recipe.

The processing time only includes the period during which the contents are under the prescribed pressure.

For instance, it takes 35 minutes and 40 minutes, respectively, to can pints of potatoes. When the canner reaches pressure, which in this case is 10 PSI, if one is below 1,000 feet in elevation, the timer doesn't start.

A beginner should start timing once the canner is under pressure, but one should make sure it maintains the target pressure throughout. An individual must restart the timer if the canner loses pressure below the desired level! That's significant since safe pressure canning calls for a period of time spent at or above a particular pressure. This is much simpler with a weighted gauge since it keeps the canner at the right pressure. One should keep a close eye on a dial gauge to make sure the pressure doesn't drop below the set level.

Unloading a Pressure Canner

To unload a pressure canner, one should first turn off the heat after the canning period is through, but should not touch anything else! In a pressure canner, an individual cannot manually release pressure because doing so could break the jars (and could cause steam burns). It can be done with pressure cooking equipment (like Instant Pots) because they have unique valves and don't contain glass jars (which aren't permitted for canning). A pressure canner should not be attempted to cool rapidly, and instant pot methods like placing cold towels on the outside should not be used.

After that, one should simply leave the canner alone until the dial reads 0 PSI (or until it has totally cooled overnight). When there is no longer any pressure, one can open the canner lid and let any remaining steam escape by releasing the vent. (Remember to open the lid with the vent released since there can be a lot of steam within.)

After that, using a jar lifter, remove the jars and let them cool on a towel on the counter. Keep in mind that the liquid inside the jars may still be boiling at this stage, given the intense heat of the contents of the jars.

Before inspecting the seals and cleaning off any debris that may be on the jars' exteriors, it is advised to let the jars cool completely on a towel on the counter. Then remove the canning rings once they have completely cooled. Whether pressure canning or water bath canning, jars shouldn't be kept with canning rings attached. It should be the vacuum inside the jar that holds the lid shut, and leaving the ring on can give the appearance of a false seal. (Because the jar is still moist from the canning process, it may also cause the ring to rust to the jar threads.)

The unsealed jars should be kept in the refrigerator for immediate use, and sealed jars should be kept in the pantry for consumption within 12 to 18 months. Various foods have been pressure canned, chilled, and had the rings taken off for storage.

Guide for Trouble Shooting

Although a beginner shouldn't have too many problems if they follow the instructions provided, there can still be a few pressure canning issues that are frequently encountered. Here is a list of the typical problems and how to fix them.

- **Siphoning or Loss of Liquid**

There are several reasons why liquid can leak out of the jars while canning. The two most frequent causes are that the lids were not secured sufficiently or that there was insufficient headroom.

Insufficient headspace can cause the meal to bubble up and strike the lid, possibly partially dislodging it and resulting in a liquid loss. Similar to loose lids, these allow the air venting from the jars as well as the boiling liquid to escape. The good news is that siphoning poses no security risk. According to the national centre for food preservation, fluid loss is only a cosmetic concern until it is "extreme," that is, more than half of the liquid is lost from the jar. There is no safety concern as long as the jar is sealed and the food is processed properly. The food above the water line may brown or dry out.

Dry beans can be difficult to can while keeping them completely below the water line, but they are still safe if canned properly. Low water levels are a common concern when canning beans since the beans can absorb some of the liquid, and one can also potentially lose liquid to siphoning.

Heat Shock (Broken Jars)

While it's possible that microscopic chips or other minor flaws in the jar cause it to break, heat shock is more often to blame. Too quickly changing the jar's temperature before the contents have had a chance to warm up (or cool down) is a reason.

It's crucial to roughly match the temperature of the food going into the canner with the temperature within the canner. Even if one heated it before pouring it into the jars, it had already cooled a little before entering the canner. If it was rawly packed, it would be much warmer than boiling, closer to room temperature. As mentioned earlier, the water in the canner should be quite hot, just hot enough to burn the hand when using raw pack recipes (around 140 F). Hot pack recipes call for barely simmering canner water (around 180 F).

Chapter 6: Beginner Friendly Pressure Canning Recipes

Here are some of the most perfect and easy Pressure Canning recipes for Beginners to begin with. So let's get into it!

6.1 Pressure Canning Turkey

Pressure canning turkey is an excellent way to have shelf-stable, precooked meat for those times when one needs a healthy supper but forgets to defrost the meat!

Prep Time: 30 minutes

Cook Time: 2 Hours

Servings: 4-6

Ingredients

- Turkey

Equipment

- Canning jars, lids, and rings made of a pint glass

- Pressure cooker

Instructions

Step 1: Set aside cleaned jars and rings. Jars should be filled with raw poultry while still at room temperature.

Step 2: Put the lids in a pot with water and heat until simmering.

Step 3: Bring water in a medium saucepan to a rolling boil.

Step 4: Cut the turkey breasts into roughly 1-inch pieces.

Step 5: Fill jars with meat, packing it down firmly with hands and leaving 1 inch of headspace.

Step 6: Fill jars to the top with boiling water, allowing one inch of headspace.

Step 7: Run a knife along the jar's interior to assist any air bubbles from escaping.

Step 8: With a cloth or paper towel, clean the rim.

Step 8: Put the lid on the container and tighten the ring with one's fingertip.

Step 9: According to the manufacturer's instructions, add 2 to 3 inches of water to the pressure canner. Water should be heated but not brought to a boil.

Step 10: Following the directions for the canner, place the jars in the canner and secure the lid.

Step 11: Once there is a continuous column of steam rising from the boiling water, set a timer for 10 minutes.

Step 12: Heat the canner continuously until it reaches 10 pounds of pressure.

Step 13: Process pint jars of boneless chicken for an hour and fifteen minutes. Then, according to the canner's instructions, let the pressure naturally drop to zero before removing the cover.

Step 14: Jars should be left to cool before being removed to finish cooling. Verify the tightness of the lids on every jar. It is preferred to clean all of the jars and lids before storing them in the pantry.

Step 15: Simply take off the ring and use a manual can opener to open the lid when it's time to consume the canned poultry. Utilizing a fork, drain the liquid and shred the meat. It's all set to go! When a can is opened, the remaining food should be refrigerated in a sealed container and used within three days.

It is usually advisable to follow the manufacturer's instructions when using a pressure canner and to check that it is in excellent working order before each use. However, a pressure canner can be used inside.

6.2 Asparagus Soup

Prep Time: 10 minutes

Cook Time: 1 day and 1 hour

Servings: 40

Ingredients

- 3-pounds of fresh asparagus

- 8 cups of chicken stock or broth

- 1 cup of shallots, minced

- 1 teaspoon minced garlic

- 1/2 t. salt

- 1/4 t. freshly ground white pepper

Instructions:

Preparation

Step 1: Get four pints, lids, and rings ready. When it's time to prepare them, sterilize the jars and keep them in hot water. Make sure to add the required amount of water to the pressure canner and heat it to a simmer.

Step 2: Each spear's woody stem should be cut or broken. Save for stock or compost unwanted items. The remaining stocks should be divided into 1/2-inch pieces. Garlic and shallots should be minced.

Cooking

Step 3: The shallots and garlic should be swiftly sauteed until transparent in a small fry pan with a minimal amount of olive oil. Avoid browning. Heat the beef stock or broth in a big stainless steel pot over medium heat. Get rid of the heat.

Filling the Jars

Step 4: Place the hot jars on a dishtowel, and then using a funnel, fill each jar with asparagus until it is 3/4 full.

Step 5: To each of the jars, add an equal amount of salt and pepper and roughly 1/4 cup of shallots or garlic. Add hot stock once all the jars have been filled, leaving 1" of headspace. If necessary, remove air bubbles and refill to the appropriate headspace.

Step 6: Using a clean paper towel dampened with vinegar, clean the jar rims of any food residue that can prevent a tight seal.

Step 7: Place the lids on the freshly cleaned rims after using the magic wand to remove them from the boiling water. Each jar's top should now have rings on it. Turn the rings to a "finger tight" closure.

Processing

Step 8: Place the jars in the pressure canner, making sure the rack is at the bottom. Bring the canner to a boil, then lock the lid and increase the heat.

Step 9: 10 minutes should be used to vent steam before closing the vent with a weighted gauge or pressure regulator (for dial gauge canner). Process quarts for 90 minutes and pints for 75 minutes at 10 pounds of pressure (11 lbs with a dial gauge canner).

Step 10: After adjusting the pressure for altitude, turn off the heat and wait for the pressure to naturally return to zero. Open the vent after another two minutes.

Step 11: After waiting 10 minutes, remove the jars and set them on a dishtowel so they may cool overnight. Till the following morning, avoid touching or moving them.

Sealing

Step 12: The jars will start to "ping" or "pop" at some point throughout the following hour. That is how the glass cools, and the lids react by being drawn into the jar for a tight closure. Some recipes could require an overnight seal. If some of the jars didn't seal, check the lids and reprocess them. To store rings, take them off.

Step 13: For a pint portion, make the soup creamy when serving. Equal to two quarts.

Step 14: Two tablespoons of Parmesan cheese and 1/4 cup of heavy cream are required for each pint.

Step 15: Add the contents of a pint jar to a saucepan, and save a few pieces for the soup's top. Stir until the soup is cooked over medium heat. Purée until smooth using a hand immersion blender, food processor, or blender. To one's liking, adjust the seasoning. Add the cream to the pot after it is back on medium heat. 3 minutes more of cooking is required. Reintroduce the reserved pieces and top with cheese. Serve hot in bowls or soup crocks.

6.3 Chicken Marsala

Chicken Marsala is a fantastic method for cooking chicken that is ideal since it starts with chicken stock as its "foundation" and thickens with cream or sour cream right before serving by reheating the contents of the jar.

Prep Time: 10 minutes

Cook Time: 1 day 3 hours

Servings: 30

Ingredients

- 5-7 pounds of skinless, boneless chicken
- Sliced mushrooms in 5 cups (2 - 20 oz. pkgs.)
- Two cups of dry Marsala
- 2 gallons of chicken stock
- 1 medium-sized onion, chopped
- 1 teaspoon oregano
- 1 teaspoon minced garlic
- Pepper and salt

Instructions

Preparation

Step 1: Remove any visible fat from the chicken before chopping it into bite-sized pieces. Set aside the minced garlic, onion, and mushroom slices.

Cooking

Step 2: Cook chicken pieces in batches in a frying pan with a tiny amount of olive oil, salt, and pepper, and then transfer to a colander set over a bowl to let the excess grease drain.

Step 3: Each pint jar should contain 1 cup of chicken and 1/2 cup of raw, thinly sliced mushrooms. Combine the diced onion, garlic, and oregano in the same pan that was used for cooking the chicken.

Step 4: The onion should be cooked until tender but not browned. In order to evaporate the alcohol, add 2 cups of dry Marsala wine, boil vigorously for 1 minute while stirring everything together, and then add 2 quarts of chicken stock.

Step 5: Bring to a boil, then simmer for a short while to let the flavours meld.

Filling the Jars

Step 6: The heated jars should be placed on a dishtowel. Fill each jar to 1" headspace with the stock mixture using the funnel. If necessary, remove air bubbles and refill to the appropriate headspace.

Step 7: Using a clean paper towel dampened with vinegar, clean the jar rims of any food residue that can prevent a tight seal.

Step 8: After cleaning the rims, remove the lids from the hot water and set them on top. Each jar's top should now have its rings on it. Turn the rings to a "finger tight" closure.

Processing

Step 9: Place the jars in the bottom of the pressure canner and make sure the rack is on the bottom. Bring the canner to a boil, then lock the lid and increase the heat.

Step 10: Vent steam for ten minutes, then seal the vent by including the weighted gauge or pressure regulator (for dial gauge canner). 90 minutes of processing at 10 lbs of pressure (11 lbs for dial gauge canner). Pints should be processed for 75 minutes if anyone decides to do so. Altitude-based pressure adjustments Once finished, turn off the heat and allow the pressure to drop gradually to zero.

Step 11: Open the vent after another two minutes. Eject the canner's lid. After waiting 10 minutes, remove the jars and set them on a dishtowel so they may cool overnight. Till the following morning, avoid touching or moving them. Inside the jars, the food can still be simmering. That is typical.

Serving

Step 12: When it is time to serve, pour the liquid into a saucepan, thicken with a cornstarch or flour and butter mixture, add 2 tablespoons of cream or sour cream and then stir in the contents of the jar. Heat until thoroughly combined. Pour some rice or angel hair pasta over the top.

6.4 White Bean Chili Chicken

Prep Time: 30 minutes

Cook Time: 4 hours

Servings: 5-6

Ingredients

- Beans

- Oil

- Chicken

- Onion

- Broth

- Chillis

Instructions

Step 1: One should start soaking the beans the night before planning to prepare the chilli. This enables them to enlarge to their maximum potential and aids in the removal of phytic acid.

Step 2: Bring them to a simmer on the stove for 30 minutes the next day, making sure they are still submerged in water.

Step 3: Prepare the remaining ingredients in the meantime.

Step 4: Set a sizable stockpot over medium-high heat on the stove.

Step 5: Pour oil into the pot, then add the chicken and toss to coat with oil.

Step 6: Cook chicken for about 10 minutes, stirring constantly.

Step 7: Stir to uniformly distribute the herbs, spices, onions, and garlic. Cook for an additional 5 minutes.

Step 8: Add the rinsed beans to the stockpot.

Step 9: Stir the chillies and broth together. Once it reaches a boil, reduce the heat to medium-low, and let it simmer for about 10 minutes.

Step 10: Heat the pressure canner on low while the chilli is still cooking. It should be at a low simmer; do not try to get it to boil.

Step 11: Remove the jars from the canner with care and pour the water into the sink.

Step 12: Evenly distribute the white bean chicken chilli among the jars using a ladle and a canning funnel (this recipe makes about 6-quart jars or 12-pint jars).

Step 13: Don't forget to divide the solids between each jar first, then fill each one with broth, leaving an inch of headspace (which means there is one inch of space in the jar with nothing filling it).

Step 14: To check for bubbles, use the canning tool or a wooden stick to run it down the inside of the jar. If required, add extra broth (or hot water) on top to maintain a one-inch headspace.

Step 15: Gently run a finger over the rim of each jar to check once more for any nicks, then use a clean cloth dipped in white vinegar to wipe the rims clean. This will assist in removing any chicken fat that could be on the jar rims from the soup.

Step 16: Top each jar with the fresh lids and secure it with bands. Each band should be fingertip tight (don't crank them on; just get them as snug as the fingertips will allow).

Step 17: The pressure canner ought to be heated up and beginning to steam at this stage. One by one, carefully raise the jars and put them into the canner.

Step 18: Attach the canning lid and tighten it in accordance with the directions provided by the manufacturer.

Step 19: Bring the canner to full, consistent steam over medium-high heat, and allow the canner to vent steam for 10 minutes.

Step 20: Ensure that one is aware of the appropriate pressure for the elevation. One can cannulate at 10 psi if they live at sea level to 1,000 feet elevation. For information on any particular canner, consult the user guide. Place the pressure regulator (sometimes known as a "jiggler") onto the vent, then wait for the pressure to rise gradually to its maximum.

Step 21: Adjust the heat gradually to stabilize the pressure until it is constant at the recommended psi (pounds of pressure per square inch).

Step 22: As soon as the canner has stabilized at maximum pressure, set the timer for the entire processing period.

Step 23: Take 90 minutes to process quarts and 75 minutes to process pints.

Step 24: After the allotted time has passed, turn off the heat and let the pressure naturally drop to zero.

Step 25: To let all the steam escape, remove the regulator or jiggler and set a timer for ten minutes.

Step 26: Carefully remove the lid and transfer the jars to a kitchen towel on a counter, where they can cool undisturbed for 12 to 18 hours, using a jar lifter.

Step 27: Before storing jars, inspect seals, take off bands, and clean them. Chicken chilli is canned and ready to be stored on the pantry shelf.

Most often, people just remove the jars' lids, pour their contents into a large pot, heat them, and then serve them with their favourite toppings, such as sour cream, avocado, and cilantro.

6.5 Beef Pie

An easy-to-make meat pie in the style of a pub that is delicious and simple to prepare. It has a top layer of mashed potatoes and is hearty and filling.

Prep Time: 20 minutes

Cook Time: 30 minutes

Servings: 4

Ingredients

- 1/2 tsp. of onion powder

- 1-liter container of homemade corned beef

- cornstarch, two tablespoons

- one teaspoon of Maggi seasoning

- Egg white, 4 tablespoons

- 4 tbsp. Parmesan (grated)

- 1/2 tsp. of garlic powder

- 500 g leftover mashed potatoes or created from scratch.

- frying oil

Instructions

Step 1: Set the oven's temperature to 200 C/400 F.

Step 2: Put the beef broth in a jug that can be microwaved after draining the beef.

Step 3: Beef broth and cornstarch are whisked together.

Step 4: Add the liquid seasoning to the broth (Maggi)

Step 5: For one minute, zap on high in the microwave.

Step 6: Remove from microwave, mix, and then zap for an additional minute on high.

Step 7: After removing from the microwave and adding the meat chunks, give it another two minutes on high.

Step 8: Set aside the beef mixture.

Step 9: Put the leftover mash in a container that can be microwaved.

Step 10: Add the egg white, Parmesan, onion, and garlic powders by stirring.

Step 11: Heat for two minutes on high in the microwave.

Step 12: Cooking spray should be used to coat a 2-quart baking dish.

Step 13: Add the beef mixture.

Step 14: To create a crust, dollop the potato mixture onto the surface in a thin layer.

Step 15: To promote browning, sprinkle cooking spray on the top of the crushed potato (optional.) Alternatively, spread butter or margarine on top.

Step 16: Bake for 25 to 30 minutes, or until bubbling hot and the crust has started to brown, at 200 C (400 F).

Serve

Immediately serve hot.

6.6 Sweet and Sour Chicken

This meal-in-a-jar recipe makes it incredibly simple to prepare dinner; all one needs to do is heat it up and serve it with rice.

Prep Time: 30 minutes

Cook Time: 1 hour 30 minutes

Servings: 5

Ingredients

- 1 red bell pepper, large dice
- Additional pineapple juice to equal 3 cups
- 2 teaspoons diced ginger
- 12 tablespoons soy sauce
- 4-1/2 pounds cooked chicken
- 8 tablespoons ketchup
- 2 largely diced onions

- 2-1/2 cups white vinegar

- 2 diced green peppers

- 1-1/2 cups packed brown sugar

- 3 ounces of pineapple chunks (cans)

Instructions

Step 1: Spread peppers, chicken, pineapple and onions in the bottom of quart jars, and then stack with more chicken on top. Tightly pack each layer until there is less than 1 inch of headroom between them.

Step 2: Dissolving the brown sugar requires combining it with tomato ketchup, soy sauce, vinegar and 5 glasses of pineapple juice in a large pot and heating it over medium heat, all the while stirring.

Step 3: Before adding hot sauce and modifying the liquid as needed, remove any air bubbles from the layered foods in the jars.

Step 4: 90 minutes of ten pounds of pressure canning.

Step 5: Produce 5 quarts.

6.7 Ground Beef Meatballs

Prep Time: 1 hour

Cook Time: 1 hour 30 minutes

Servings: 2

Ingredients

- ground beef

- water

- herbs

Instructions

Step 1: Combine ground beef with the dry herbs and seasonings of their choice, including salt substitutes, oregano, marjoram, parsley, ground black pepper, onion powder, and garlic powder.

Step 2: Meatballs can range in size from 3 to 4 inches.

Step 3: A small amount of fat or oil can be heated in a skillet by spraying it with cooking spray first.

Step 4: In batches, brown the meatballs in the skillet, then remove them to a covered bowl or pot to maintain their heat.

Step 5: Loosely fill hot half-litre OR heated one-litre jars with meatballs.

Step 6: Leave a headspace of 3 cm (1 inch).

Step 7: Fill jars to the top with a boiling liquid (stock, tomato juice, or water from a kettle), leaving a headspace of 3 cm (1 inch).

Step 8: Adjust headspace by DE bubble.

Step 9: Wash the jar rims and attach lids.

Step 10: Processing pressure: 10 pounds weighted gauge, 11 lbs dial gauge; when over 300 m/1000 ft, adjust pressure for altitude. Half-litre or 1-litre jars should be cooked for 60 or 90 minutes, accordingly.

Chapter 7: Other Methods for Preserving Food

Food preservation refers to the management and treatment of food to prevent or significantly slow down deterioration brought on by or accelerated by microorganisms. In order to preserve food, it is typically necessary to stop the growth of bacteria, fungi, and other microorganisms, as well as delay the oxidation of fats that lead to rancidity. Inhibiting natural ageing and discolouration that might happen during food preparation, such as the enzymatic browning reaction in apples after they are chopped, is another aspect of this. Any chemical ingredient and/or technique that, when applied to food, delays changes brought on by the development of microbes or makes it possible for the physical characteristics, chemical composition, and nutritional value to be untouched by microbial growth might be considered a food preserver.

7.1 Freezing

Simply place the extra in the freezer—how that simple freezing can be!

Food freezing is simple for beginners because it doesn't require much-specialized equipment. Most veggies need to be blanched or cooked before freezing. This halts enzyme activity and guarantees high quality.

What does blanch mean? When vegetables are blanched, the cooking process is stopped by heating the vegetables before submerging them in cold water. The typical blanching period is three minutes in hot water.

Fruits are frozen with sugars or with antioxidants to prolong storage and prevent fading. Some people like to freeze meals on a cookie sheet for fruit and vegetable preservation before putting them in vacuum-sealed containers for long-term storage. Vacuum-sealing frozen produce helps prevent the production of ice crystals and can increase the shelf life of frozen items by three to five times. Without vacuum sealing, no one rarely actually stores anything in the freezer.

In short, freezing preserves the food's current components, including vitamins and enzymes. However, they will deteriorate in the freezer over time. One will need an additional freezer or freezers if one wants to use freezing as a major component of their food preservation strategy, particularly if they intend to freeze whole tomatoes, peppers, or eggplants.

When freezing food, it's preferable to use three bags and to push out as much air as possible. The prevention of freezer burn will be extended through this. Food flavour and nutrition are both diminished by freezer burn.

Glass jars can be used to freeze food, but it's important to be aware that they are fragile. Especially broad or regular mouth Mason jars with curved shoulders, which are vulnerable to freezing. Straight-sided speciality freezer jars will perform better.

If someone does freeze food in Mason jars, make sure the food is kept sufficiently below the level of the shoulder so that it can expand in the freezer without reaching the jar's shoulder.

Finally, some items don't freeze well, including cooked rice, sour cream, and cucumbers. However, many things can be frozen, including jam, fruit, cheese, butter, dough, unbaked bread, etc.

7.2 Dehydrating

One of the earliest forms of preservation is dehydration. People are effectively retaining the food's current nutrients, including vitamins and enzymes, when they dehydrate it. It might, however, deteriorates over time, particularly if not preserved properly. Dried foods have a wide range of shelf lives; some only last a few weeks, while others, like dried beans or grains, can last up to 15 years. Store dried foods in dark, cool, dry, and pest-free areas for optimal performance. It is preferable to have consistent cool temps in comparison to changing ones when it comes to temperature. Meats can rarely be kept for an extended period of time unless they are low in fat and thoroughly salted, and even then, they benefit from cold storage.

When dried and then rehydrated, several foods lose some of their pleasant texture. Examples include fruits and vegetables like bell peppers and cucumbers.

Users still need room for dry meals even if they are considerably lighter and smaller than fresh ones. This includes shelves, pantries, bins, and/or buckets containing desiccant packets that absorb moisture so that food doesn't spoil.

7.3 Fermenting

This category includes processing dairy into cheese, making homemade vinegar or alcohols, chocolate as well as Lacto-fermentation, which produces foods like cabbage or pickles. This is the oldest and healthiest technique of food preservation in use today, aside from dehydration.

Fermentation converts low acid foods into high acid foods, extending their shelf life for storage or enabling water bath canning as opposed to pressure canning. Food ferments when salt or particular starter cultures are added. This makes it more nutritious and easier to digest. "Live culture food is another term for fermented food.

Because of acidity and bacteria pre-digesting the meal, flavour and texture alter.

The healthiest way of food preservation, fermentation, boosts nutrition by producing more probiotics, enzymes, vitamins, and healthy acids. The healthy acids work as a preservative and are good for the intestines.

Even when users ferment their food at room temperature, but still need to move fermented items like cabbage or pickles into cold storage, like a refrigerator or cool basement, once they are finished. Storage at room temperature is not an option.

Even though ferments are good, and although packing anything into a jar with salt and letting it rest is one of the simplest ways to preserve food, it can be harder to get a decent result in hot summer temperatures over 80 degrees Fahrenheit.

7.4 Preserving in Salt and Sugar

Before contemporary canning, freezing, and dehydrating were possible, food preservation in salt and sugar was more popular. Sugar and salt cause food to lose fluids. The growth of microbes is hampered by this. Like humans, bacteria and moulds require water to grow.

For individuals with adventurous palates, salt and sugar preserving are handy because they substantially alter flavour and texture.

A fun approach to quickly preserve fresh herbs is by using salts and sugars infused with herbs.

7.5 Immersion in alcohol

Alcohol, like salt and sugar, sucks water out of food, preventing the growth of microbes. Small portions of food will last virtually indefinitely if thoroughly submerged in the hard liquor of one choosing. Avoid attempting to preserve too much food in insufficient alcohol. The amount of water that can be absorbed has a maximum.

Making flavour extracts and preserving foods with a high acid content, such as fruit, are best done with this method of food preservation.

7.6 Pickling in vinegar

Rapid pickling, often known as vinegar pickling, is a quick method of food preservation. Vinegar preservation, which includes immersing fruit or vegetables in salt or vinegar, requires high-quality products and processes. In addition to preserving the meal, the addition of veggies and vinegar gives it crispness and tang.

Vinegar can be used to preserve food without heating or canning since microbes cannot survive in an environment with high acidity. Imagine a vintage pickle barrel. Vinegar has a long history; evidence of its use dates back to about 3000 B.C. in Egyptian urns. It was formerly known as poor man's wine because it was a sour liquid created during the fermentation of wine. The Old French word "vinaigre," which means sour wine, is also where the name "vinegar" originates.

It is most likely that vinegar was first used to preserve food in northwest India circa 2400 B.C. It developed as an easy method of food preservation for long voyages and export.

By using vinegar to preserve veggies, users obtain a cuisine that only requires a few basic components and can be stored for a very long time. Simple science preserves food with vinegar. Vinegar's acetic acid effectively slows spoilage by killing off any microorganisms present, and it also helps vegetables maintain their acidity. However, there are a number of limitations to vinegar pickling. Really important is the acetic content. Vinegar should never be diluted. Acetic acid is effective at killing bacteria and also acts as a barrier against botulism.

There are several recipes available for pickling. Pick one and then adhere to the guidelines. There are other factors to think about in addition to a decent recipe. Use food-grade plastic, stainless steel, or enamelware when making glasses. Never use copper or iron because they will make the pickles discoloured. Make sure there are no chips or cracks in any jars. To check the temperature of the water, use a candy or meat thermometer.

If the recipe calls for it, people will need a water bath canner that will enable them to cover the jars in water. In addition, one will need a rack or some towels for the base. Use only the cleanest, freshest produce. The product keeps its shape best when it is a little under-ripe. Only use fresh spices. Salt substitutes cannot be used, only food-grade salt. Use granulated or beet sugar instead of brown sugar whenever necessary. Use 1/4 less honey when using. While lime will add a pleasant sharpness, some recipes call for alum or both; neither is actually necessary.

7.7 Dipping in Olive Oil

Although this technique for preserving food at home is widely used across Europe, experts would certainly not recommend it to a beginner. It is submerged in oil to preserve food, which keeps out the air. Vegetables with low acidity provide a major botulism danger.

There are two downsides to this method. When consumed, the oil won't be completely removed from the meal because it will become saturated with it. If people consume an excessive amount of foods preserved in this method, we run a great danger of consuming too much fat. However, consuming more fat shouldn't be a problem when working under strenuous conditions or during periods of intense physical activity.

Due to the high cost of oil, particularly olive oil, which is recommended and best for this procedure, this method of preservation may prove to be rather expensive. In the Mediterranean nations, where oil is readily available and reasonably priced, the approach employing olive oil is widely employed.

7.8 Freeze Drying

Food preservation at home is now possible with freeze drying (lyophilization). How do home freeze dryers function?

First, purchase a powerful freezer which can withstand temperatures as low as -30°F (-34°C).

Second, every time users use it, simply combine this with a chamber that is totally airtight and can maintain a vacuum without oxygen.

The third step is to connect a high-end vacuum pump with enough suction power to pull a zebra's stripes.

In order to repeat the sublimation process for hours on end, one should add a heater and thermostat in the fourth step.

Fifth, connect a humidity sensor to confirm that the water is off and start the cycle.

Many goods that cannot be preserved using conventional techniques, such as dairy products, whole meals and leftovers, can be preserved at home using freeze drying. Vegetables, fruits, meats, and seafood can all be stored.

One may manufacture a product of excellent quality by gently drying food at home. Food drying is the least destructive method of food preservation when compared to canning and freezing, all of which need extremely low temperatures.

Fermented foods have a reduced shelf life, yet fermentation provides nutrition. Foods that are dried can be stored for many years and take up very little room. Use dried foods as snacks or in soups, stews, and other dishes where they will benefit from slow, protracted cooking with lots of liquid. Use within two to three years.

For beginners, freezing is simple, but freezer space is needed. Food can last for two to three years if vacuum sealed. Food should be consumed within a few months if it is not vacuum sealed.

Foods that have been freeze-dried are kept at room temperature, not in the freezer, and they can last for up to 20 years. Oily or fatty foods should be consumed within five to ten years.

A wide range of foods can be preserved with canning, although it does call for specialized tools. It's advisable to use canned goods within one to two years.

Regardless of the home food preservation technique anyone selects, properly ripened produce that is rapidly collected and processed is probably more nutrient-dense than the majority of grocery store options.

At least two considerations are very important when selecting the best food preservation methods for the family.

The storage capacity comes first. For instance, freezing or fermenting could not be practical if users don't have a second refrigerator or freezer, at least on a large scale. The space and appliances immediately restrict the alternatives.

Secondly, the tastes of the family. It would be pointless to preserve food in this manner if the family doesn't like fermented foods or the texture of dry meals and won't consume them. Some people are concerned about ferments' alcohol levels for health or religious reasons.

It is tastier, healthier, and less expensive to use a variety of methods, including canning, than to rely just on the grocery store, especially if one buys in bulk or when the food is not in season.

Make the greatest choice keeping family in mind!

Conclusion

The most adaptable form of preservation is definitely canning, which is such a terrific skill to have. With the help of canning, one can use the excess green beans and cucumbers from the summer to make a range of delicious pickles and relishes that every family will appreciate, ranging from tart dills to sweet gherkins. Alternately, make delectable jams, jellies, and butter using fruit that has been foraged, gathered from the garden, or purchased at the market. The process of preserving and handling food prevents or delays food decomposition, loss of quality, edibility, or nutritional content and enables prolonged food storage. Preserving entails delaying the oxidation of fats that can get rancid as well as inhibiting the growth of bacteria, fungi like yeasts, and other microbes.

People who used to can and preserved their own food have largely disappeared thanks to modern technologies. Modern transportation has made it feasible to walk into a grocery store just about anywhere in the nation and acquire just about any type of produce in the middle of January. Previously, food was preserved to be able to enjoy it later on during the year. Simply put, this was unheard of decades ago.

Food has been preserved by humans for generations. It was how our ancestors survived. Most individuals no longer need to preserve their food thanks to contemporary technology because they can buy practically any variety of produce at their neighbourhood grocery shop.

It's not as difficult as it seems to preserve one's own food, whatever the motivation. Knowing a few fundamentals will keep everyone on the right path and ensure the safety of the meals. One of three techniques—drying, freezing, or canning—is used to preserve food. The greatest preparation goes into canning, and it's really not that difficult. Simply described, it's a method of food preservation that involves heating food inside a sealed glass canning jar and releasing air to seal the jar. By stopping the deterioration, this technique renders the food shelf-stable. Water bath canning and pressure canning are the two types of home canning.

With this guide to canning and preserving, anyone can easily prevent any product from going to waste. Don't throw away any produce. Home cooks can experiment with items that might not be in the supermarket and know exactly where their ingredients are sourced because of their affordability. Review these fundamental process instructions and a guide on canning and preserving to assure food safety if one has never tried these at home.

Printed in Great Britain
by Amazon

30329076R00040